The Things You Cannot Change

Isaiah R. Hicks

BookLeaf
Publishing

Presentation by *BookLeaf Publishing*

Web: www.bookleafpub.com

E-mail: info@bookleafpub.com

ISBN: 9789395950633

First edition 2022

For You,

Whose eyes are a mystery,

Whose life guides my pen.

Living in the Town of McKenney

You walk by the old bank, watching a cracked reflection
Mimic the sad posture of the oak tree growing
Sideways over Sunnyside Elementary.

People who live here know the roads
Better than they think know each other,
But it's okay because you heard
Jenkins' Mini Mart by the church won't card you.
People like your father pay the lottery there
Like it's a bill.

You enter the Dollar General on Doyle
With a hoodie on, eyes following you
Through the aisles because someone
Shoplifted a box of Hot Pockets
From the frozen section yesterday.
If you text a girl you dated in high school
To ask why her father wouldn't shake your hand,
She'd spare your feelings.

The only things moving here are
A Ford that carries a doe in its deathbed
Or the memory of your brother flipping
His first car after falling asleep at the wheel.
A man who wasn't your neighbor
Woke up your family in the dead of night.

You don't remember why you'd catch the school bus
At the trailer park some mornings.
You only remember the friends you made there.
They would play kickball with you
On Sunnyside's playground until sunset.
They would shake your hand.
Good could only be found in them,
The bus driver who'd cook deer jerky for you,
And the sky you still miss seeing each night.

You get a drink from the mart and sit
Outside on the sidewalk. The emptiness
Of your wallet presses into your thigh
And the little, paper slip of a Pick 3 laughs
At you, again, for being late on your light bill.

When another Ford drives by,
You see yourself in the buck they hunted,
Black eyes reflecting the image of you
Praying under the shadow of Big Bethel.

Self-Portrait Concerning a Name

And I have never understood my own name,
The way it starts with a selfish letter,
Concurrently defining someone
Writing a poem about himself and,
In Hebrew, that "God is salvation" when my
Pastor, deep-voiced and stern, gives a sermon
Saying *all thy children shall be taught*
*Of the Lord** while the children entering
The Congregation Hall, after leaving
Sunday School, are laughing at a girl
Named Blake because a boy
Named Jordan says she has a boy's name—
A mother who named me
Isaiah
Because she found herself closer to God
After the accident of my conception,
Praying now during a hymn my father is singing
With the men's choir—*At the Cross*—
People clapping along, children giggling
At Blake, a woman crying
For the child she lost yesterday,
All nameless if not for our need of labels;
My exhales spin on an air we have named
Wind
When the idea of identity—not just my own—
Becomes too much for me,
I pray with eyes tightly closed

And the backs of my hands face the soft,
Church floor that rests under blue pews growing
Empty
When the children of God close their eyes
For the last time, their names soon lost
And never again spoken.

In the end,
Even if my name will be uttered in church,
Will they still remember who *I* was?

* "And all thy children shall be taught of the Lord;
  and great shall be the peace of thy children."
—Isaiah 54:13, KJV

Fear

No, there aren't enough colors
In the rainbow for her, so you
Remember when she would add
Streaks of brown in her coloring book.

You called your mother the other day,
And you asked about your niece.
The kid does gymnastics now,
You know. Robotics, too.

You don't pray enough for your niece,
Nor for your sister. The lack of
Animosity only wedges the guilt
Deeper into the folds of your brain.

You tell yourself you are never
Too busy for family, but you check
Your calendar to see if that's true.
This kind of feeling burns like

The July lightning your niece
Pointed out to you some years
Ago. She said it looked scary.
These days, is she still scared?

You don't want to be the father
She doesn't have, but feeling absent

From even her life makes you
Wonder what kind of uncle,

What kind of brother,

What kind of son you are.

To Be Rendered Naked
(On Being Home II)

No,

You do not know from where the words
Will come, or when. There has been
An intermittent heaviness all day that
You have been all too afraid to confront.
Sure, when you came home, your dog
Was happy to smell you, his tail flailing
Madly. The soft whimpering. He is old.
His fur has yellowed; his vision, worsened.

Truth be told, you have never been happier
To be home. Something is missing, though.
You feel that there has been a shift.
Your niece asks you to record her jumping
In a pile of leaves, and all you can think
About is how bereft you will feel once
The house you are standing next to
No longer has people to call it home.

Your mother and father's
Recent lab results. Despite seeing mostly
Green values, you cannot help but think that
By the time you are able to understand each
Metric, it will be far too late. Dust the shelf

Of family pictures. You get sick of how Time
Yearns to eat everything, to degrade. Delete.
You apologize to God for forgetting His grace.

Autumn has an austere way of rendering things
Naked. Out here, the stars are so easy to see
In the cold mystery of night. You used to
Point out constellations to your parents,
Orion readying his bow as you try to point.
They never knew where you were pointing,
But they always said they could see it, too.
If you could, you would give them the stars.

Tomorrow morning, you will leave again.
It is okay. You have been worrying that
Spending so much time away has weakened
Whatever attachment you have with home.
While being here shows you parts of yourself
That you have routinely forgotten,
It also makes cozy the four rooms
Of your heart. You are reminded that, at home,

There is more.

Self-Portrait Concerning Sight

Can she see me?
I am sitting outside at the Virginia Museum
Of Fine Arts facing a maquette of Neptune
Palming a sea turtle,
Dolphins curling around him.
Staring at Neptune staring at a wall.
Fish are his clothes.
O, to have dominion over the seas—
Over anything. Maybe she'd see me then.

When I learn how to swim, her and I should go
To the beach and head far out into the Atlantic.
The shore has never been my thing,
But I can make do with sand castles.

Or maybe we ought to hike,
Smell of oak and basswood floating
So intimately around our noses.
Does she want to read poetry at the summit?

I haven't written for her in so long.
That is probably the reason why
She has yet to see me.
Challenging for a poem to work for the writer
When all there is to write about
Is someone else.
Turn my hand over and it will

Still want to hold hers.
Soft of my palm welcoming her entirely.
Curve of her waist, smooth of arm,
Leg bend, and jaw to cheek.

My goodness, what season is this?
I have never known a spring to be this warm.
This heart-caressingly

Warm.

I drop my shoulders, exhale.

An embrace evolves when one cares.

Family cares,
But sometimes I forget this.
Can they see me?
A good family is one that will still love you
When you don't visit often anymore.
Time is quite rude, and all too often,
It moves too fast for me.

My father spends hours a day
Trying to figure out what lottery numbers
He should play that night. Is it too dark
On the road when you go to the gas station?
Can you see?
Does that midnight raffle yet butter the bread?

I remember coming home and seeing
The swing set that he built was gone,
Reduced to a heap of lumber in the backyard.

I pray that the cancer doesn't return
Because I don't know what I would do,
Futile human that I may be,
If my father was reduced
To a heap of bone that way.

Should he end up somewhere like
Bon Secours, I want him to remember
How to find syllables
So that he may speak with me.
There will be more than emptiness
And cold between us,
If I have anything to do with it.

I will have the strength to reconcile his end,
Any end,

But how will I see myself?
Better yet, how do I appear now?
The maquette of Neptune sits in water
That is not calm, my reflection undulating
Against a heaven that melds
Blue of hydrangea and orange of melon.

I suppose whenever I see myself,
The real image, without my glasses,
Is a blur.

Though, when I can't see,
It is the Lord who leads the way.
O, how these lilies are dressed in splendor—
What better clothes does He give to me?

Let me help you view this wonder.
All of these sparrows serve as proof,
All of the globe flowers blooming,
Expanding the image of the world.

And you, reader, what do you see
Besides the canvas of this page
And the ink that decorates it?
Are the letters painting a portrait
Vividly enough? To your liking?
Marvelous how these little shapes
Dance into words in the silent voice
Of your mind,
But the dance your thoughts will create
Because of my language
Is unbeknownst
To me.

To me,
Drawing this image of the self
Is enough sometimes.
I turn to face the wall that
Neptune is facing, and I breathe.
I can see nothing on this surface but
Tiles and roughness of texture.
That is all.

To Remember the Sun

You'll walk outside to remember the sun
On slow-turning days like this.
It's too cold to sit in Monroe Park.
Something within you will suggest
Walking to Belle Isle, the place
She wanted to go for the anniversary.

No use in going home yet.
You left your apartment key
On your desk, next to the watch
She gave you for Christmas,
The face of it still glistening in that
Shade of green you like so much.

Walking to Oregon Hill gets you a spot
On a bench that overlooks the James
And the railroad below. You throw a rock
At one of the train cars to remind yourself
That you can. You think the wind blows
For the same reason. She would agree.

You'll write a poem about the walk
After you sit on a rock by the river.
If you could go anywhere else,
You wouldn't. No other place is good
Enough to watch water flow
In ways you will never understand.

How freeing it may feel to be this river,
To be connected to everything.
If she were here, she'd lay her head
On your shoulder and appreciate
The smallness of being human with you.
You'll finish the poem, and you'll sigh.

Where Have You Been?

1.
What do you remember?
Waves curling up at your feet
And receding with that Atlantic inhale.
Saltwater sensations decorate that
Mental image. The cruise ship off-shore
Is whispering its farewell on the wind.
The sunset looked different then,
Somehow warmer. Enveloping.
Nothing written in the sand can stay,
But the memory will be with you forever,
No matter how worn and disjointed.
If you knew that would be the last time
You saw her, you would have danced
In that room with her just a little longer
Under the whir of the fan.
Soft sway catching the rhythm
Of a song you can hardly remember.

2.
You remember being lost,
Telling yourself to take deep breaths as
You sit alone on a rock at the riverbank.
There are chuckles from a couple
In the distance when they speak
About dancing. Lapping river water has
Never been so quiet and comprehensible.

A mosquito buzzes by, but it ignores you.
Cast another stone into the James.
It does not skip on the water,
But merely splashes and sinks instead,
The way you intended.
Aimless, you try to reconcile
That nagging, unlabeled feeling.
Even if formless, it will always be real.
The real question was not
Where are you going? But rather,

3.
Where have you been? You ask yourself.
Sometimes you sit in the murk
Of your bedroom, ceiling fan whirring.
Its bulb cover was never fastened correctly,
So you can see a pile of dead gnats
Only when the light is on.
There's a live mosquito trapped, too.
You forget the question
On account of the buzzing.
How did you get here?
You do not remember opening
The window, nor noticing the mosquito
Until now. You wonder if it could dance.
If so, how gentle would it sway?

Portrait of My Muse

But the more I write, the more I want
To take up all of my syllables, my words,
And make your face out of the letters.

The painting above my bed does not show
This face. What wonder is it to question
The structure of an expression, of a face

That I have never seen nor will ever speak to?
I know you have eyes that are full of living hymns.
You must have once felt the calm part of sky

And made it back down to earth again,
Unfettered. Great drop of water that you are,
Tell me about the cloud you once slept in.

And the rest of you? Tell me if your hands
Ache at the roughness of writing your ideas,
The movement of a wrist and fingers all too

Complex for those less occupied with
The want of writing something, anything.
Anything that can say what it was like

To have breathed a mountain, the weight of it.
What it was like to have seen a hollyhock reveal
Its dark halo to the stranger of midsummer.

To have heard the first musings of your mind,
Loud song of how the world should be.
To have been dwarfed by the size of everything

And nothing. To have had nothing. To have
Once slept in nothing. To have dreamt.
To have opened your eyes in a mess of a bed,

Sunlight still sliding through the open parts
Of your blinds. Your body lying still,
Face turned from the man who painted you

And left whatever expression you might have
Had become a mystery to me. Or perhaps,
Ever so calmly, your eyes are still shut.

If so, to me you are always resting,
Dreaming up the possibility of anything as the
Painter captures the artwork of you.

I Am Writing This for You

There are many people out tonight,
And you wonder if any of them are sad
That the cicadas have stopped singing.

If you like the way traffic signals look
On the sidewalk at night, let me tell you
That the ones at the intersection
Of Boulevard and Main have been red
For far too long.

Something about the smell of rain
Is what gives you the courage to thank
God for this world in spite of the stones
Scattered at your feet.

I am writing this for you—
You, who are always concerned
With the way the days turn over too
Slowly, the way the leaves brown
Just a little too quickly
In the first exhales of October.

If the newness of the moon
Makes it too dark to see
Where you have been on this walk,
Remember, please,
That it will not always be night.

Self-Portrait Concerning Longing

At times, I feel that I move through life
Doubled over, hunched animal that I am,
Fearing that I will one day become rabid.
Rapid is the way the food in my fridge
Seems to grow old. I learned to climb
Out of myself long ago, but it is something
I cannot do correctly. When I ask God how often
I am going to feel this way, I am only told
To continue seeking Him. Sometimes,
I forget that I am not alone. Who else?
Who else is much too lazy to fold whatever
Clean laundry sits in a pile in their room,
The problem of dirtiness dealt with already,
But the remnant of it laughing in your skull?
No matter how clean, it was once dirty.

No matter how clean, you were once the same.
However, you, too,
Have found your spring, graceful as
The hydrangeas that unfurl their little
Petal-fists in a flurry I will never understand.
My God, why would I ever let you go?
Or at least, the idea of You.
You, you loud and lovely aubade,
Should experience every season, every
Twisting breeze, every low tide with me
So we can see Mother Earth's expression,

Dimples and all.
When?
When will my windows fly open
At the wind of You?
Let the water slip by your fingers
And remember how gentle the world aches to be.

Neon

While walking down Broad Street at night,
You start to think of the way you used to write.
The way you would write about people—how
You no longer write about some of them anymore.
You let the night air carry your words farther
Than thcy would ever be able to fly when
Sent on the carelessness of your breath.
This sidewalk decorated by wet leaves
And cigarette butts will never know what it is
Like to not be walked all over.
Concrete and neon signs without neon have
Never meant more to you than they do tonight.
Walk under some scaffolding
And ask yourself if the workers who placed
It there are leading lives of contentment.
You are not sure what became of the man
Who asked you to buy him food at the corner
Of 3rd and Grace because you were not sure
Where your next meal would come from either.
This cold air and rolling leaves do not bode well,
But this night will soon be a memory—
One of moonlight and solitude.

Black Dog

Someone's trash got caught in the wind.
You sit in the park and a passing
Thought tumbles into your head.
It does a pervasive dance
Like the wilting daffodils, an elegy.

You shake your head, but not because
Of the gust whipping your face.
Whatever you have yet to reconcile
Is hardening with age.

But existence is law. This new and
Strange feeling should be illegal.
Someone passes a little too closely
Behind your chair, but when you turn
Your head, the park is empty.

All except for the black dog walking
With a limp across the street,
One ear missing, frail body trembling,
Ready for the next nobody that walks
By to give it whatever is left of lunch.

Lo, this creation is heaven-sent and *gentle*.
Your eyes are beholden to the
Network of living branches above you.
The dog would not understand.

Sometimes, you wish you were simpler,
A plastic bag tumbling in mulch, the
Thank You! on its side rolling with laughter
In the wind because none are welcome.
You sink into your chair.

Wanderings, like Ice

1.
You decide to go for a walk
On this winter night
Because you can,
And that is the only justification.
Settle your nerves. The ice will continue
To creep even if you are inside.
The same streetlight will blink itself
Into darkness, and, no, the roads
In Richmond will not improve.
And that is okay.
The only worry you have is the
Human one that wears your jacket,
Zipper catching on the fabric
As the cold saps the dexterity
From your hands. It is on nights
Like these when the hymn of poetics
Makes you feel less forgotten by the light.
You walk by your job and are thankful
That you did not have to work today,
But remembering your rent
Almost makes you feel a bit emptier.

2.
You trip. You stumble
Over bricks forced out of place
By the roots of a spiteful tree,

Lack of life hanging from its branches.
Never before has the mortality
Of anything (especially your parents)
Been more apparent to you than now.
The longer you walk these frozen
Sidewalks, it becomes harder
To understand how time solves
Anything. Autumn, sadly, makes
More and more dead leaves.
You grew tired of time some time ago.
Your mind settles on the world again—
The homeless man whom you cannot
Help is sleeping on the bus-stop bench
At Harrison and Grove. You shiver
And wonder if the bus stops
For him at all because you have
Seen it ignore him once before.
He was awake then.

3.
You think you must have been chosen
For this kind of isolation.
You are not sad, only introspective.
Looking inward is your way
Of building meaning for yourself
Before you are reduced to bones.
As you make your way back home,
Your reflection greets you across
The street on Gilmer, the moving

Silhouette of a person whose mind
Has too many living ideas sleeping
Inside it: the beauty of the capacity
To love, the throbbing poetry
Of a toothache, pulsing at the root,
Just as sensitive to cold as you are, etc.
You know life will be different one day,
But it is the magnitude of change
That creeps around in the back
Of your head, behind everything else,
Like the ice you step over
Before finding home once more.

Cage

I walked to Lombardy Market for a Mexican Coke
And kept the bottle cap in my pocket.
When I left the store, I watched
The branching shadows dance on cement.
Leaves painted in moonlight
Bade me farewell and sang
In their carotenoid language
About an existence which I could not understand.

While crossing the street, I thought about the way
We humans see dead leaves and misremember
How alive they once were. Facades of reds
And yellows were blinding once.

These trees, during autumn,
Seem as alive as those chlorophyll hearts
Struggling to beat against their delicate, veiny cages.
Let the sidewalk be their cemetery—
What a funeral we live in.

The deep hum of a car engine
Stopped me from jaywalking,
Lost in thought.

❖

I counted the hours of the night
While I spoke to myself about writing
For the children whose only conception is a thought.
Those unborn cannot enjoy
The simplicity of swings
On Park Avenue's playground.

Playgrounds are nocturnal,
And it is its silhouette,
Its adherence to the unknown,
That threatens the children of The Fan.

Innocence is stolen from Youth
When dead leaves pile at the bottom of a slide
In one muddled mess of dead things.
Sometimes, this world is no place for a child.

As I continued,
A sedan slammed on its brakes at the crosswalk.

I walked Laurel and watched a lonely Kroger bag
Filled with the wind of ideas
Tumble across the asphalt.
A raindrop landed on my lips when I wanted
To see if God was watching.

Has the sky kissed me?

I dream of making the unknown feel familiar,
The way, during a night that is new to this body,
An old coworker walks by me on the sidewalk
And has forgotten my name.

When I am able to show
How a poem can speak,
No,
Breathe,
Like the exhale of a tree's blossom,
Will I have freed my song
From this cage of language and flesh.

I walked back to my apartment
Rolling the teeth of a bottle cap
On the tips of my fingers.

Headlights illuminated the newness of my spirit
When the wind no longer needed to fill me.

The Things You Cannot Change

Can you smell it? There is something
Riding on, yes, writhing in the air
The way cold passes through the holes

In your jacket. It looks a lot like
The streetlights do not know whether
To be on or off, and what's worse?

They do not have a choice in the matter.
Neither do you when the car before you
Does not stop at the 2nd Street light

And nearly collides with the fire truck
Flying down Broad. God has quite
The way of watching over each of us.

You chuckle, and you can see your
Breath right before you ask yourself
If the things you cannot change will

Grow brittle and dusty or become
Something you do not understand all
On their own. That tight feeling in your

Heart when you realize all you can do is
Wait is enough to make you pause and
Sit at the bus stop, clutching your chest.

You will not board the bus that comes.
You are not sure if that matters, though,
Because as you are sitting here for

A little while longer, one hand gripping
The bench, the smell of the burning
Complex down the block refuses to ask

Whether or not you can catch your breath.
You are not sure if you have a choice
In the matter. And that, that is worse.

The World Turns Lonely in the Cold

You wonder if the wind has always felt
This bitter, the way it grazes your neck
As you step into the world once more.
The moon is curious, watching you walk
To the 7/11 on Grace in the silence of night,
Wanting to ask if you feel as lonely as you look.
Dead leaves sit in their concrete pews
And think about what it meant to be noticed
For the first time at summer's conception.
Now, it is winter, and the 7/11 cashier
Does not care about the leaves she swept up
Earlier, nor about the ones that entered with you
On frozen air when you opened that door.
People kill for this kind of monotony.

On your way home, you walk beside the sound
Of your footsteps that fill Grace Street
With their echoes. The car that turns before you
Onto Laurel does not stop for you,
Nor does this great Earth. How did you get here?
A dented paper plate passes on the wind.
The beat-up Toyota Camry in a parking lot
Sits alone, paint chipping off its hood,
Under a blanket of creeping frost.
Walking down Laurel, you start to think
About what your life will slowly become
While leaves, unnoticed and innumerable,

Come and go with the seasons. You look up,
Hoping to see *more*,
Something you have never seen,
Something that would resemble
Your idea of the glorious face of God.

Becoming Unnamed

You let fester all the things you can't
Be bothered with, so you press on,
Iron-footed and slack, the name
For this feeling always escaping you.

A poet you do not know died today
Because of ice on the roads.
Her funeral will be next week.
You will not be there, so you write
A poem about her. Her family
Will never read it. You're sure she
Was a loving daughter and friend.
Probably a loving mother, too,
But her newborn wouldn't know.
Tell him when he's old enough.

If the snow waits for no one,
Then why should you?
Get in the car and drive for as long
As you think you need, those
Roads of snowfall will only become
More difficult to travel alone.
Rend yourself from the clutches
Of some cold, far-off sadness,
For that is not what you feel today.
A totaled car greets you
On the interstate. Its distracting,

Confused position troubles you.
Whoever died in that crash
Will, in time, become unnamed.
You figure you could end up
Like that, too, if you pass soon enough.
If this roadway, this icy asphalt,
Were not named, it would still exist.

Everything is everything,
Even without its name—
From this cage of metal that could
Careen on sheets of frozen water,
To this miracle vessel pushing
Crimson life throughout your body,
A flow as ancient as the water
Of the Euphrates that now falls
On next week's ceremony for the dead.

The Fox

As you walk by the river today,
You can overhear everything, but
You are not listening. The water
Has never looked more incomplete
On a windy day like this. You cannot
See the bottom of the river when
You kick a rock into the current.
Wonder if you will see it downstream.
What could you be thinking about?
It is those trees that stretch over you
To look into your cluttered headspace.
Do not question why the fox drops
A squirrel carcass at your feet or
Why you stand frozen at the sight of it.
There is something you want to say,
But you are not saying it. Your words
Tell you everything but the truth.
The fox does not stay to listen,
And the trees are ignoring you, bare.

Fall of Leaves

Better to go outside and stare at the sky
Than try to translate the riddle of TV static.

But you do not know this,
Nor if the fan above you will do
Anything other than whir.

Separate from yourself
Like two bored lovers
And push the dead weight
Beneath your bed.

You were entertained once,
The schema of your life
Dotted with periods of commotion;
Now, there are only periods.
Punctuation.
Full-stops of anything
That piques even the mildest
Or wildest of curiosities.

Sway with the trees to pass the time
And pray the leaves don't fall too soon.

Decline

Hold onto this feeling just a little longer
To bask in the faux newness of truth.
One night, you sit on your porch
In a town nobody visits anymore and
Stare at the water tower that
A man drowned in two years ago.
Just like him, nothing is left of you.
Even the moon has the time to pity.

The only fun to be had is at the bar
On Carlyle where the waitress
Remembers you fondly. But you,
You always forget her name the
Moment you step foot inside,
That old, creaking wood wedging
Itself into this forgotten and solemn space.

When the tourism stopped (and you
Could no longer sell souvenirs)
You asked yourself if anything was
Worth it anymore, not knowing
How to simplify a complicated
Answer to such an inevitable question.

A friend of yours has been playing
The same lottery numbers for five years

Since he was released from prison.
You ask him why, his reason giving way
To gradual shifts in detail and meaning.
Perhaps, this is because you are forgetful,

Or, more likely, that you do not care.
Each night, the tree in your front yard
Reeks of crow shit while their obsidian eyes
Seem to peer into your broken window.
They caw. They are laughing at you.
Somehow, you find the courage to sleep.
The thought of leaving prods at your spine.

But why would you go when you
Have nothing left to take with you?
Why cut ties with the waitress
Or leave your dear friend behind?
The only souvenir anyone needs from here
Is a crow's egg crushed beneath
The boot of a man who dreams only
Of the water tower and whiskey.

Piece of You

What you lost is beside you now,
Sitting in the cold air at your feet.
It is something indiscernible,
Like a pit in your stomach
Or a long sigh. The rain is not
Falling hard enough to wash
Away your shadow of concerns.
Sometimes you pause and ponder
The beauty of a song that sings
Of the world caving inward
On itself, ingesting this
Patchwork of rock and dirt
As the stars trend rapidly away.
This is solitude.
If you could, you would bury
Your possessions in your backyard
Beneath the hanging, wet branches.
That tragic bark.
Anything to widen such a
Threadbare frame of mind.
Listen to the rain.
How formless are these lights?
How heavy is the weight that
Sits in your tired heart?
Remnant of what you once were
Staring up at you, from the puddle,

Its reflective eyes watching someone
You have never seen before.

Made in the USA
Middletown, DE
06 February 2023

24196456R00031